From the very early childhood, Lika Gorsky surprised everyone with her drawings.

At the age of three, she created original portraits of amazing likeness of everyone in the family.

At the age of five, she began to sculpt small complex sculptures of people, trees, flowers, and baskets of fruit.

When Lika was five years old she won an admission to the prestigious Art Studio for Gifted Youth at the Pushkin State Museum of Fine Arts. There young gifted artists were taught by renowned art professionals.

By the age of six, Lika showed an interest in architecture. She began to draw blueprints of houses, streets and squares. She was fascinated with urban planning as well as the complex distribution of utility networks.

At the age of six, Lika was one of the youngest students to be admitted to the Junior Division of the Moscow School of Architecture.

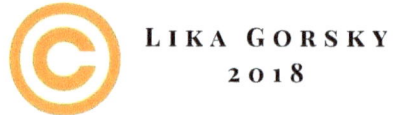

Lika Gorsky
2018

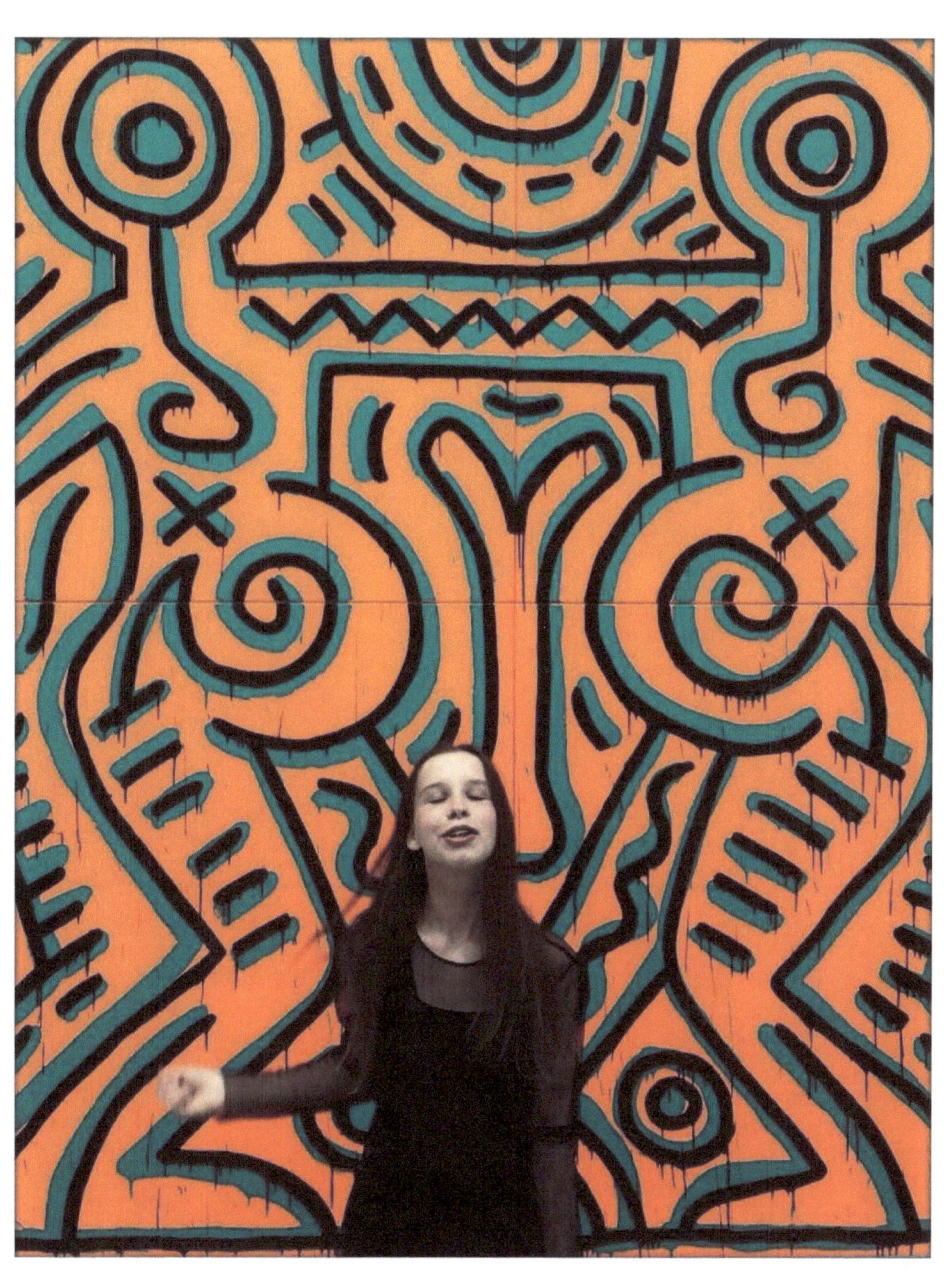

Lika Gorsky

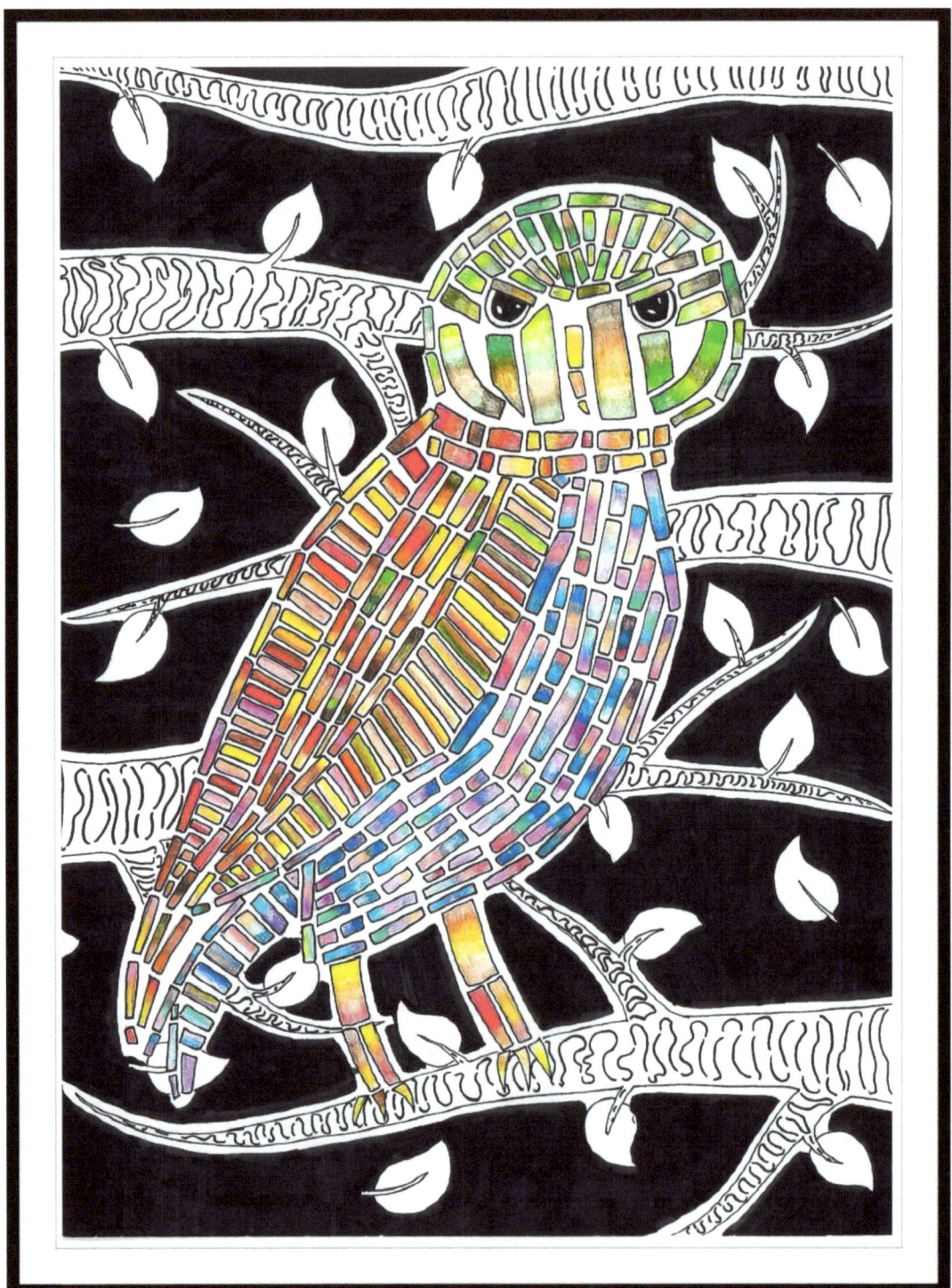

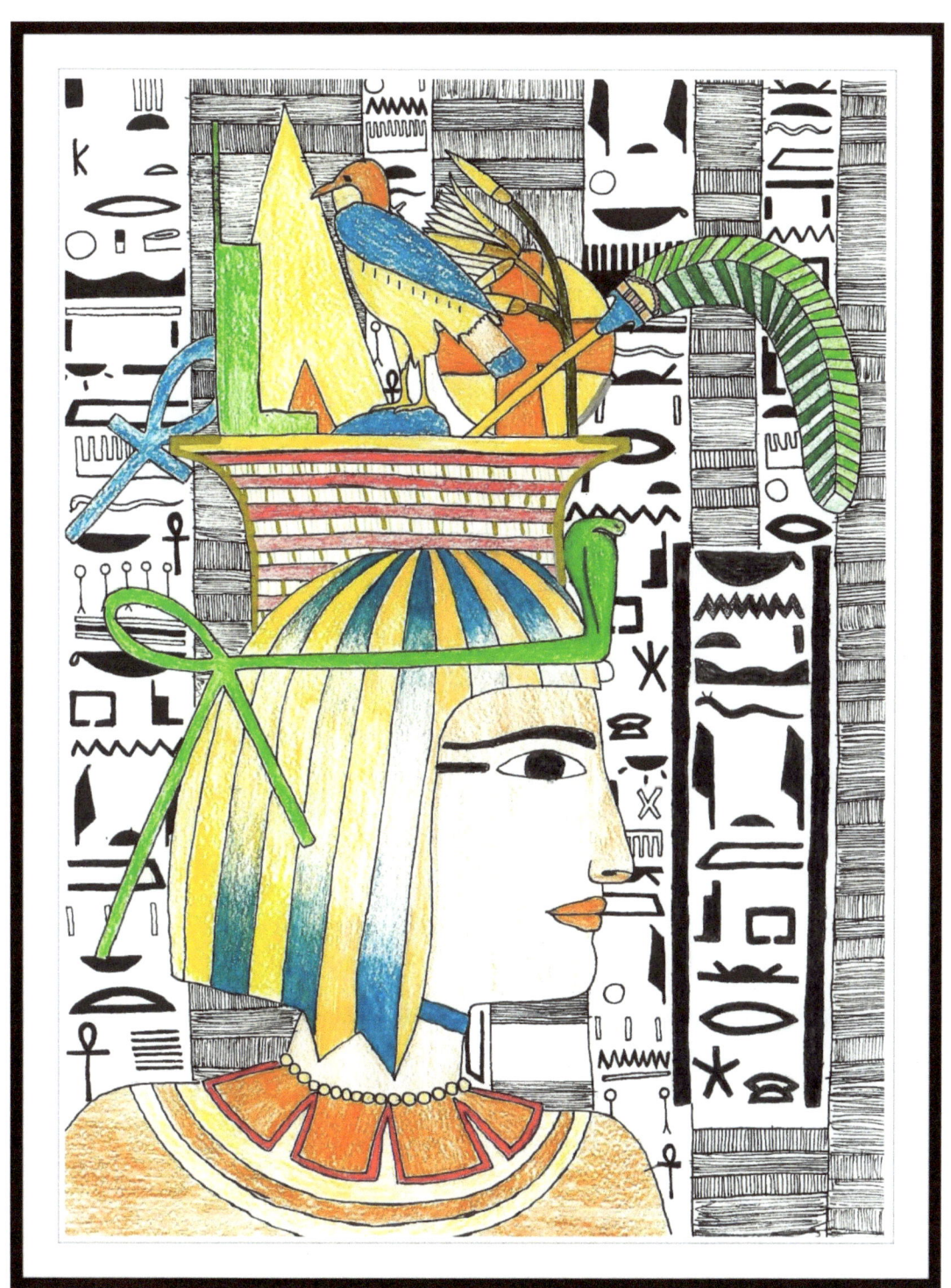

CLEOPATRA

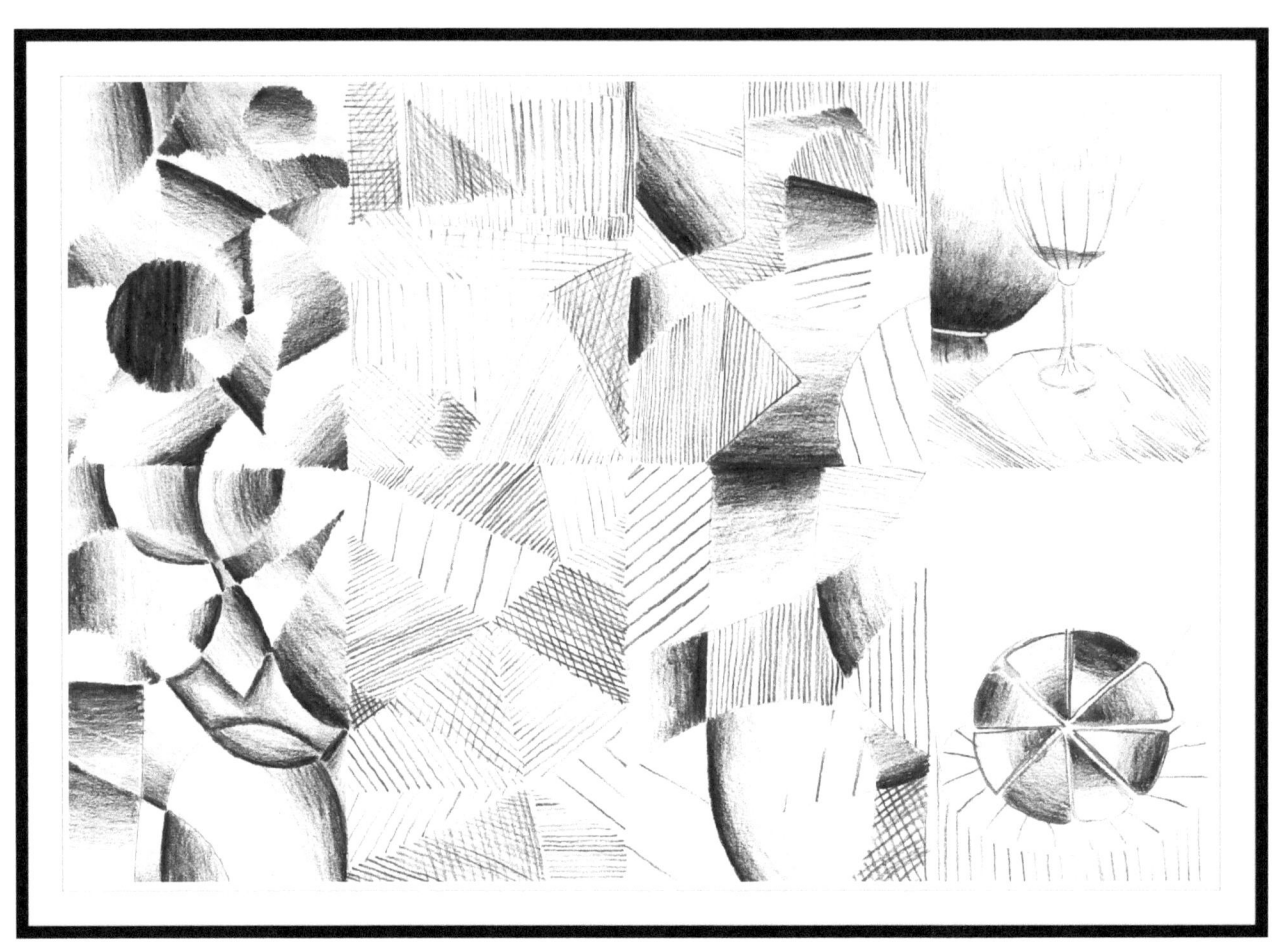

LOUD

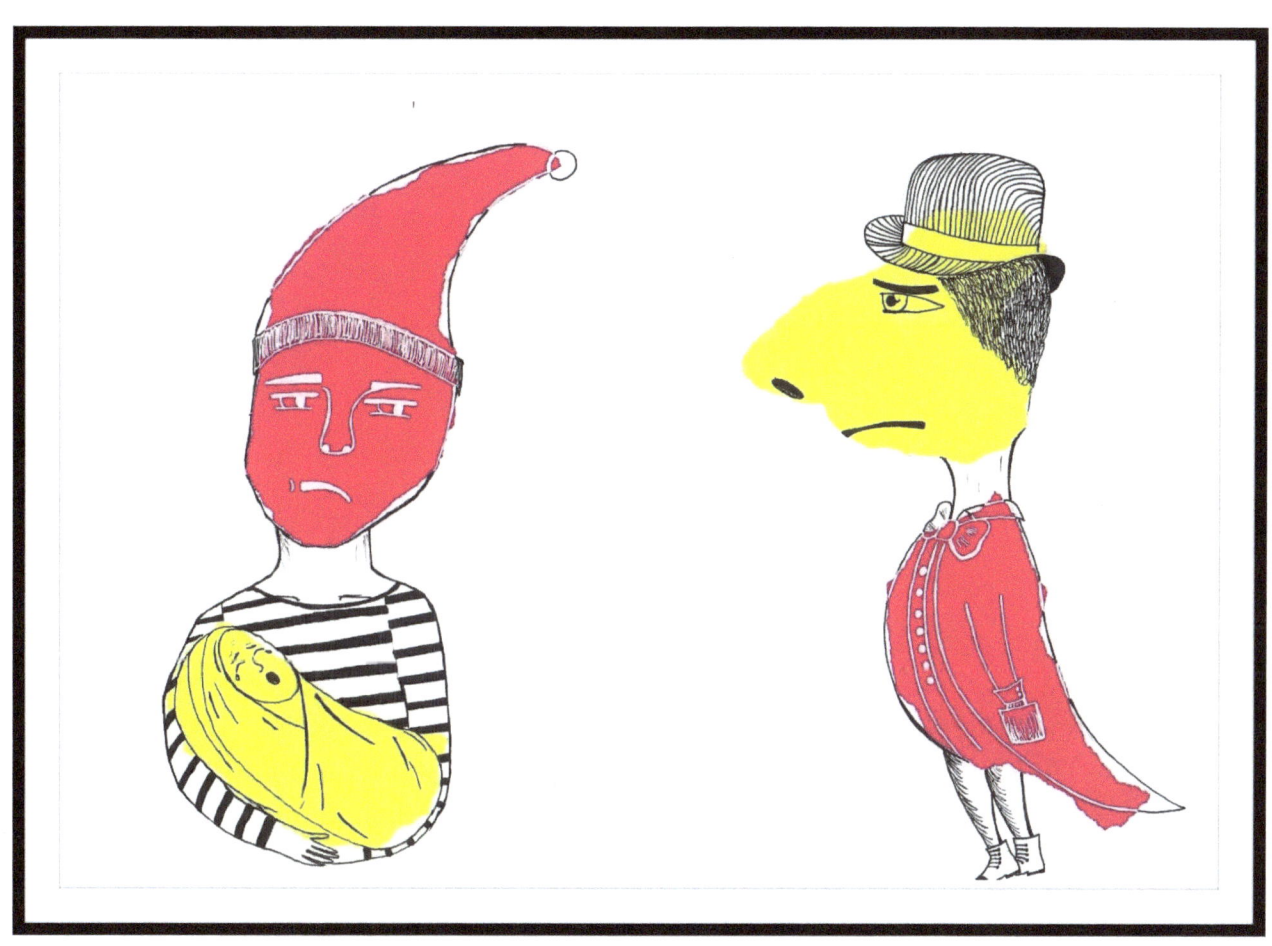

The Brown's Family

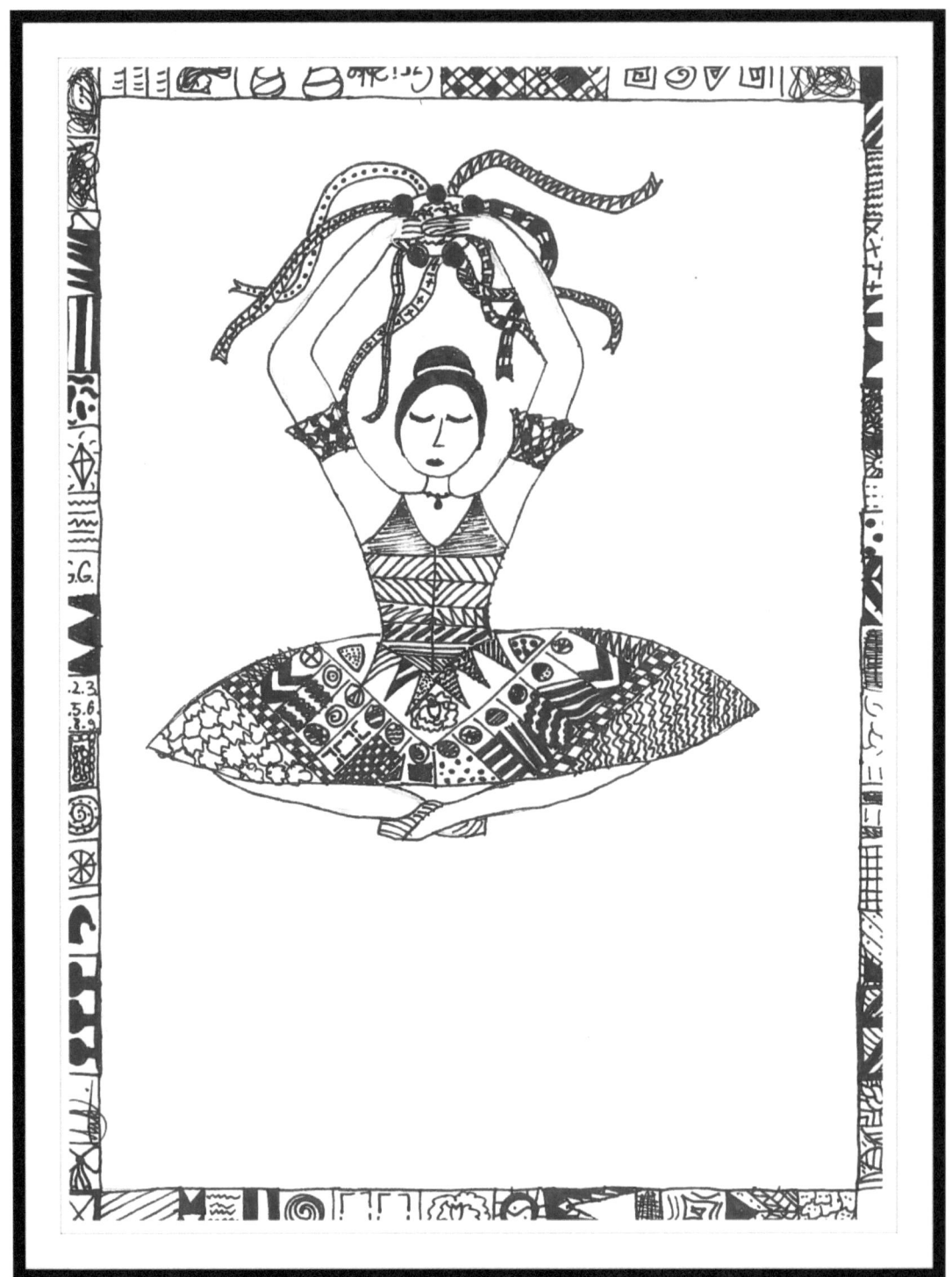

FRANCESCA

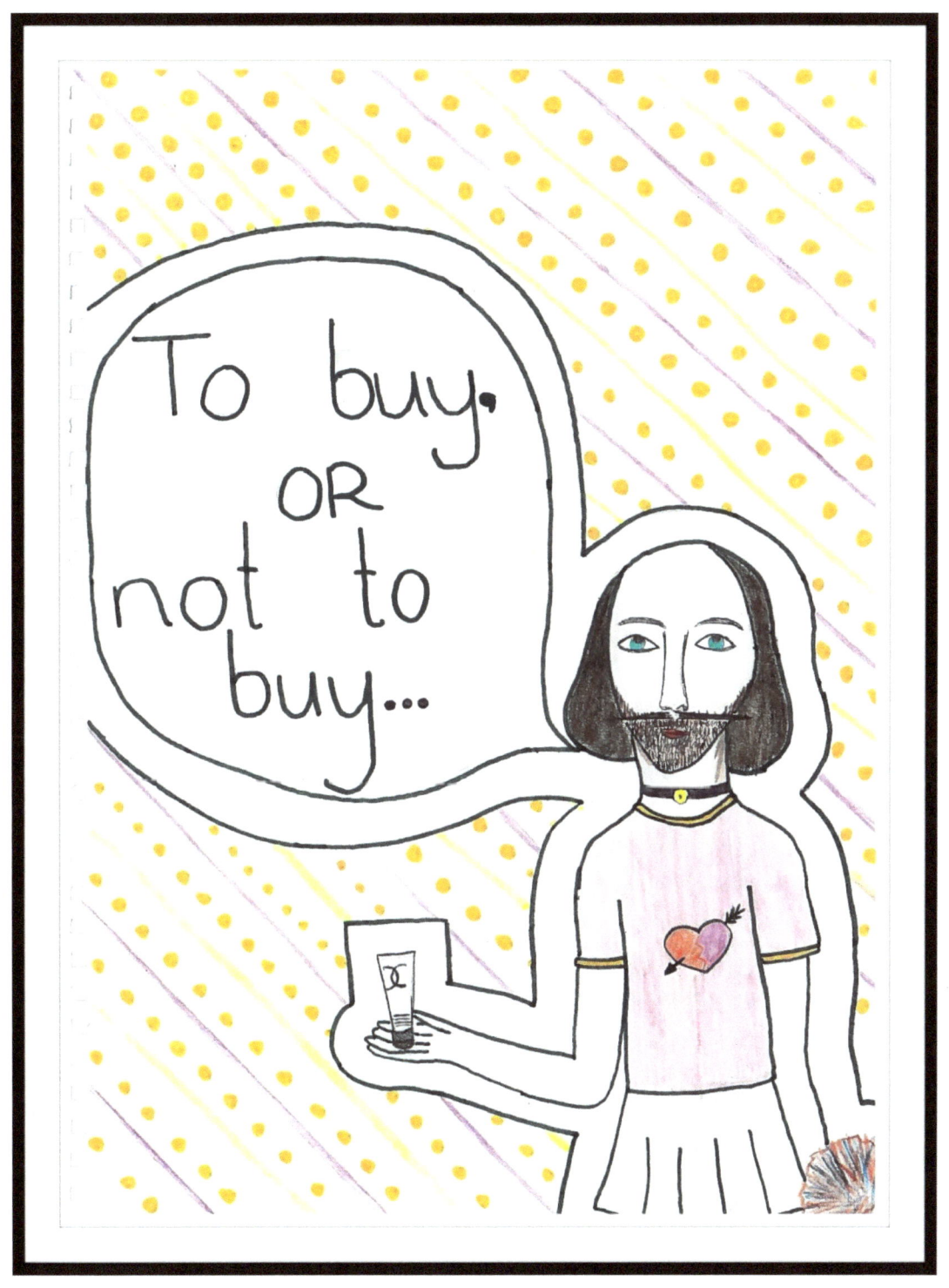

The Meaning of Life

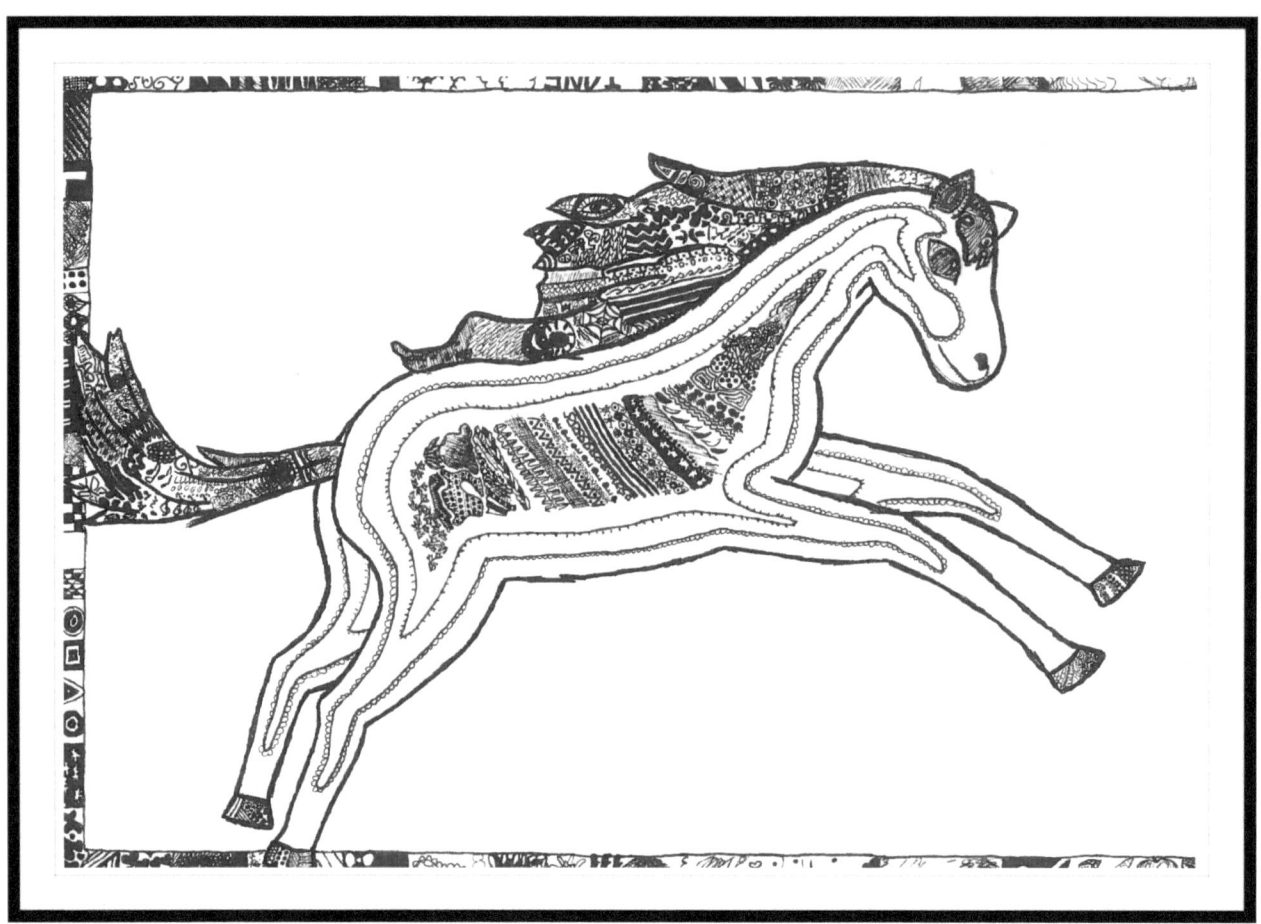

A HORSE

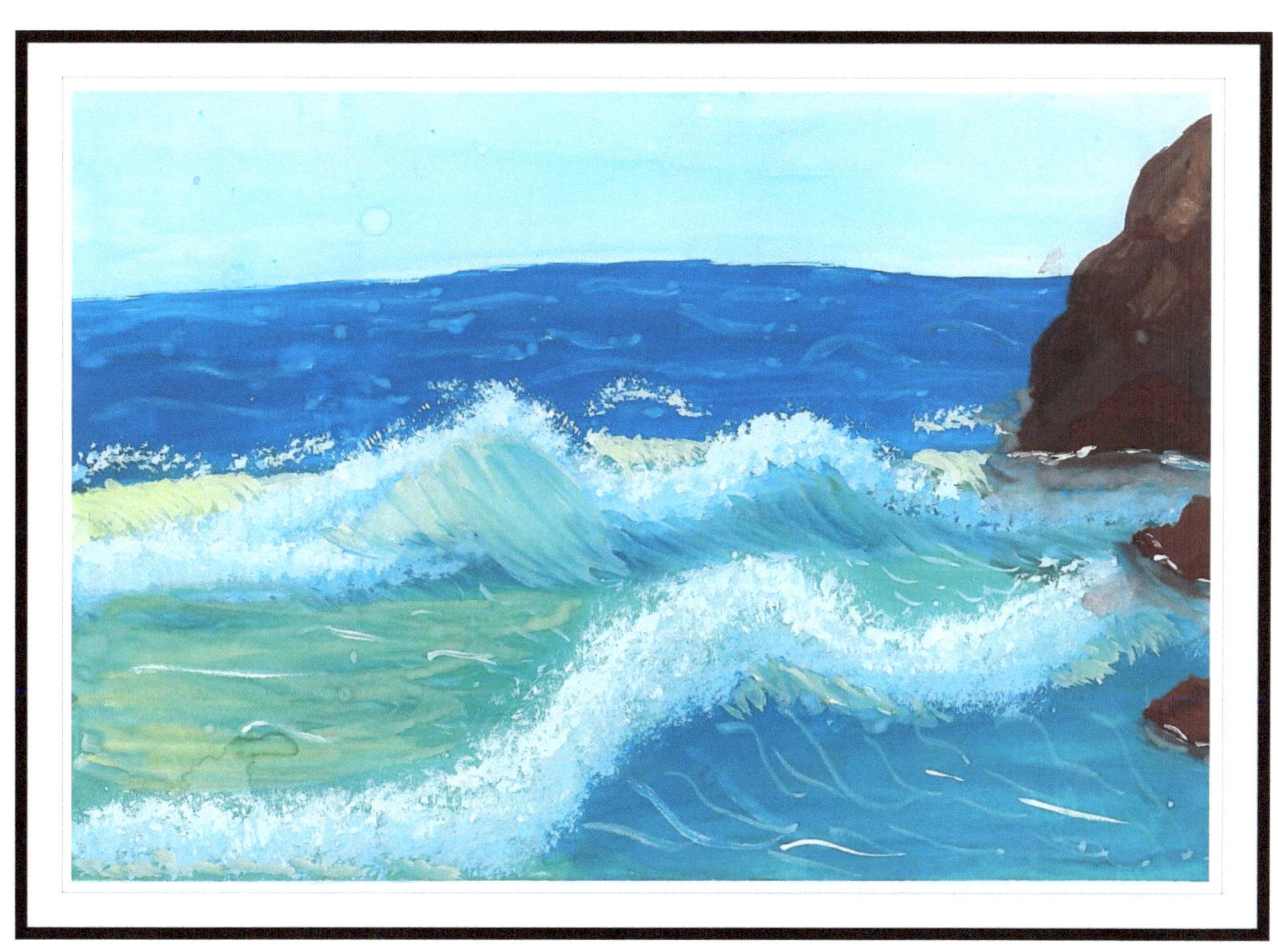

A Summer's Day

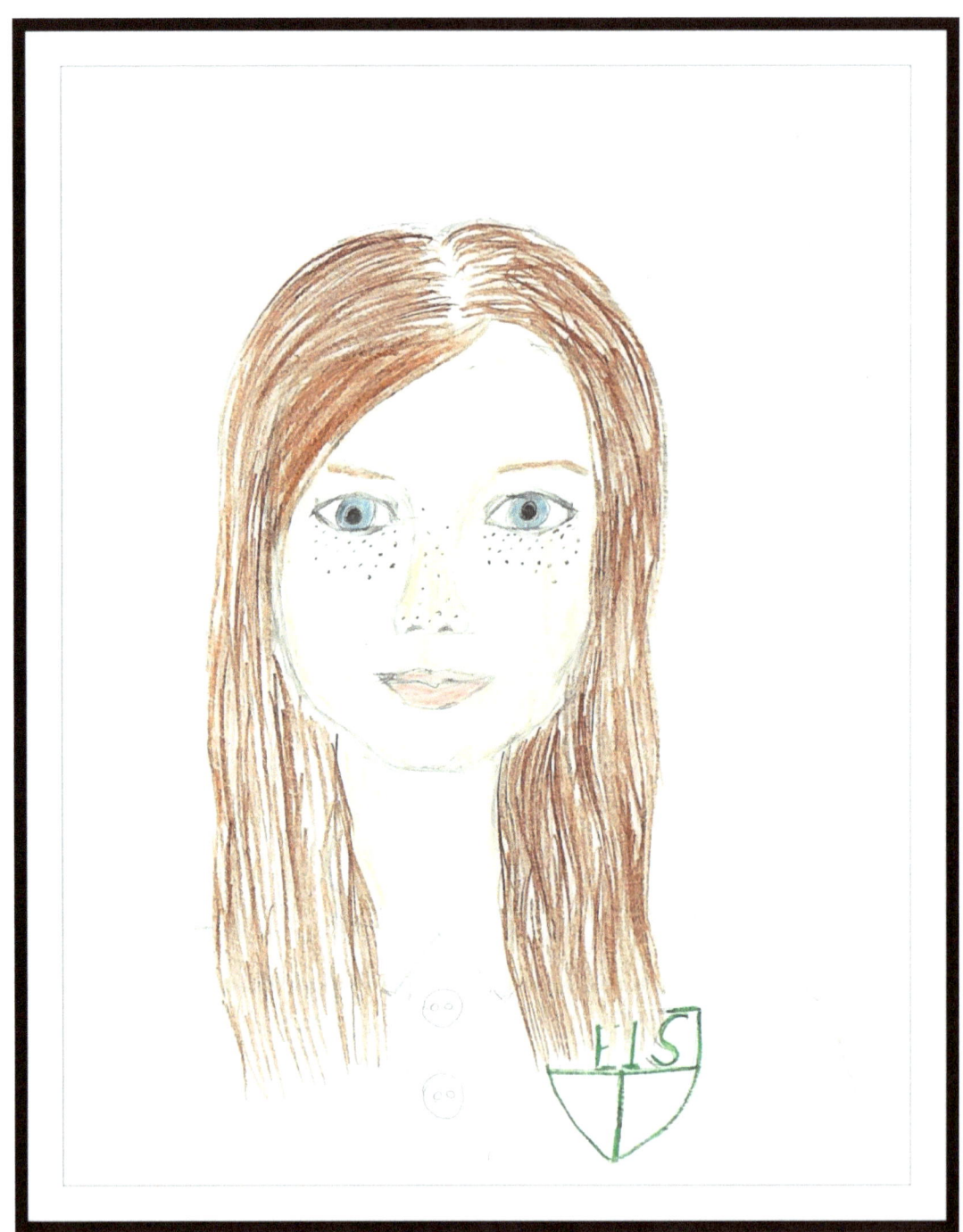

Selfie

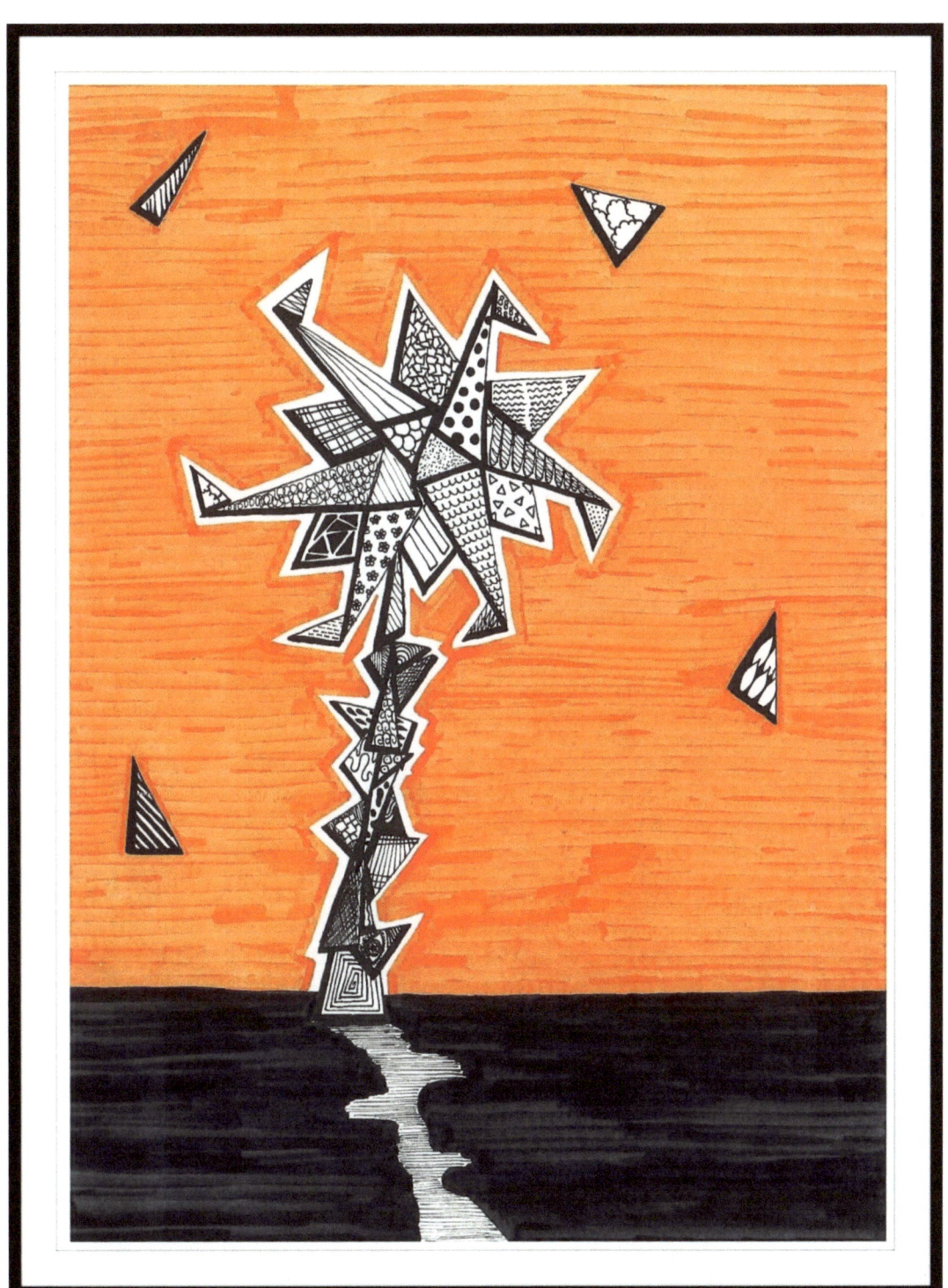

Sample 37

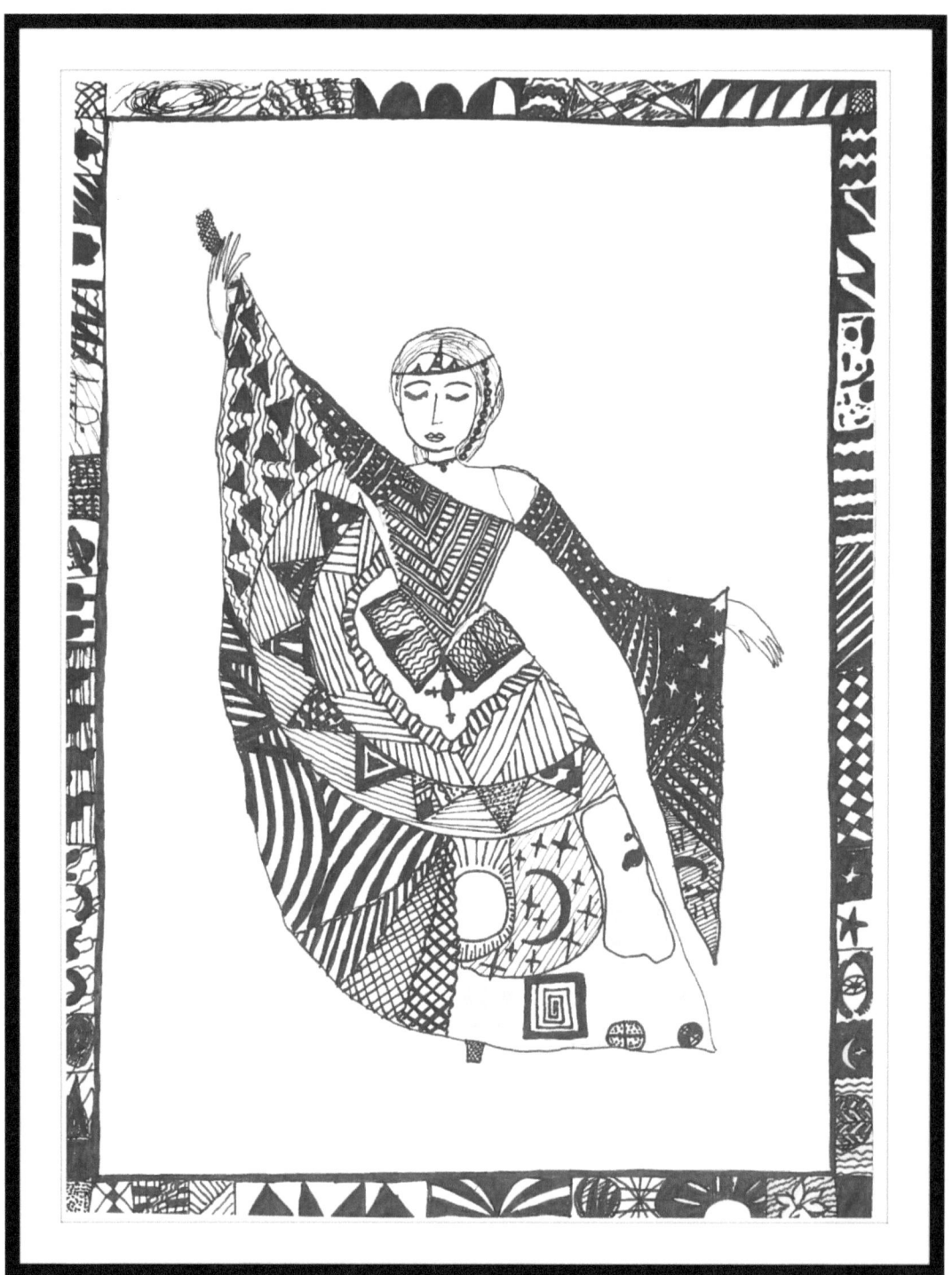

OPHELIA

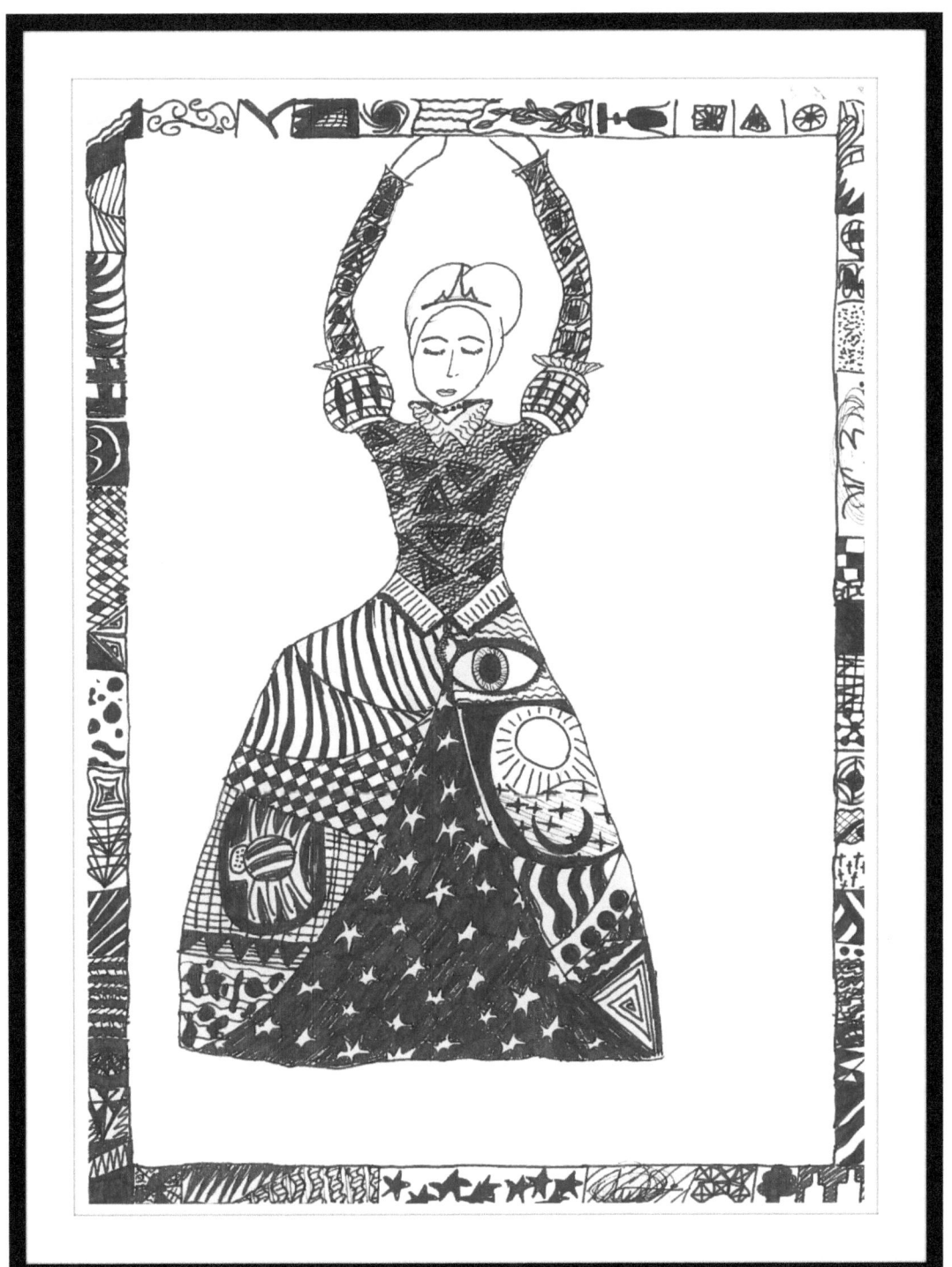

GEORGIA

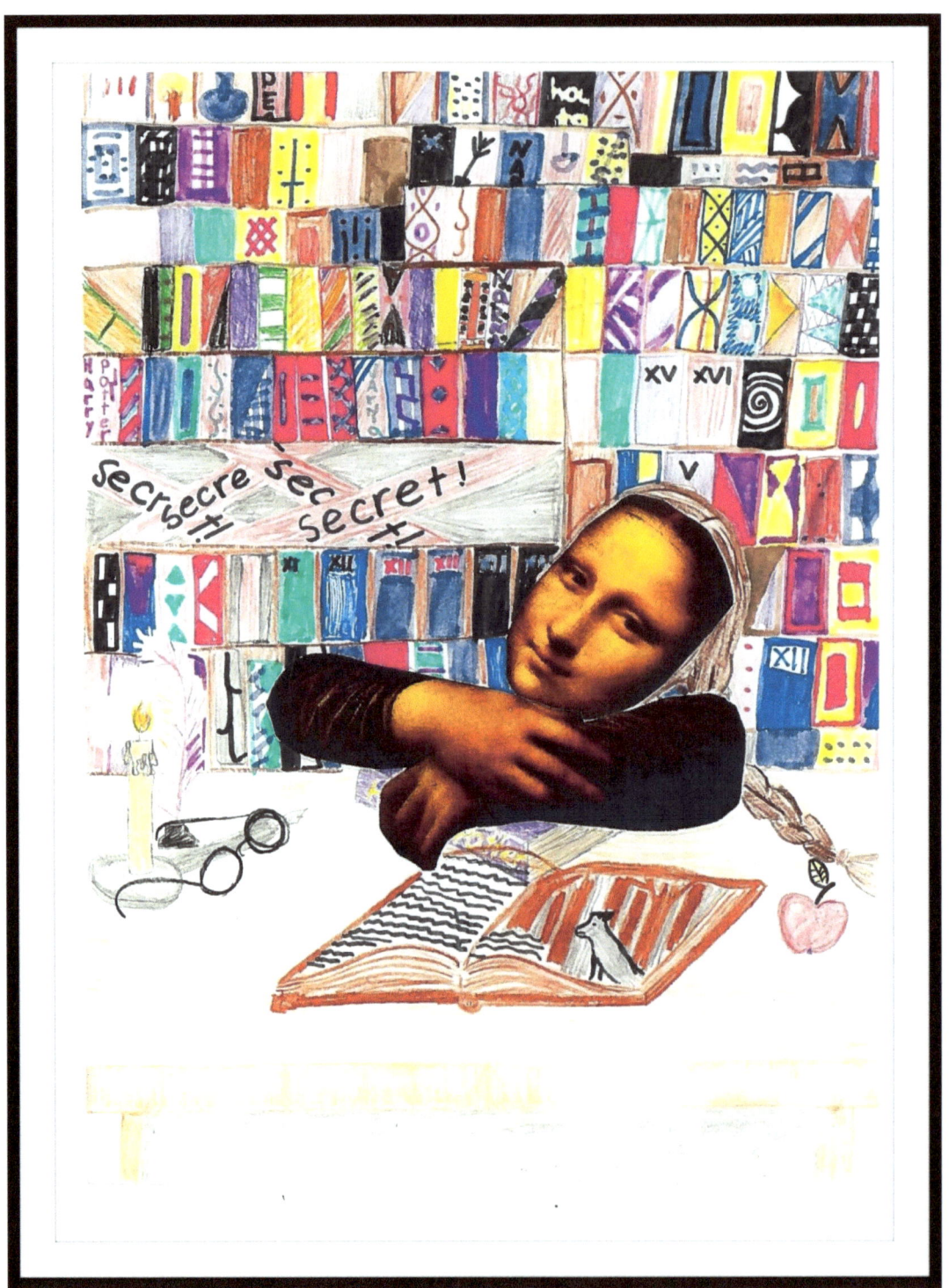

HIGH VALUES

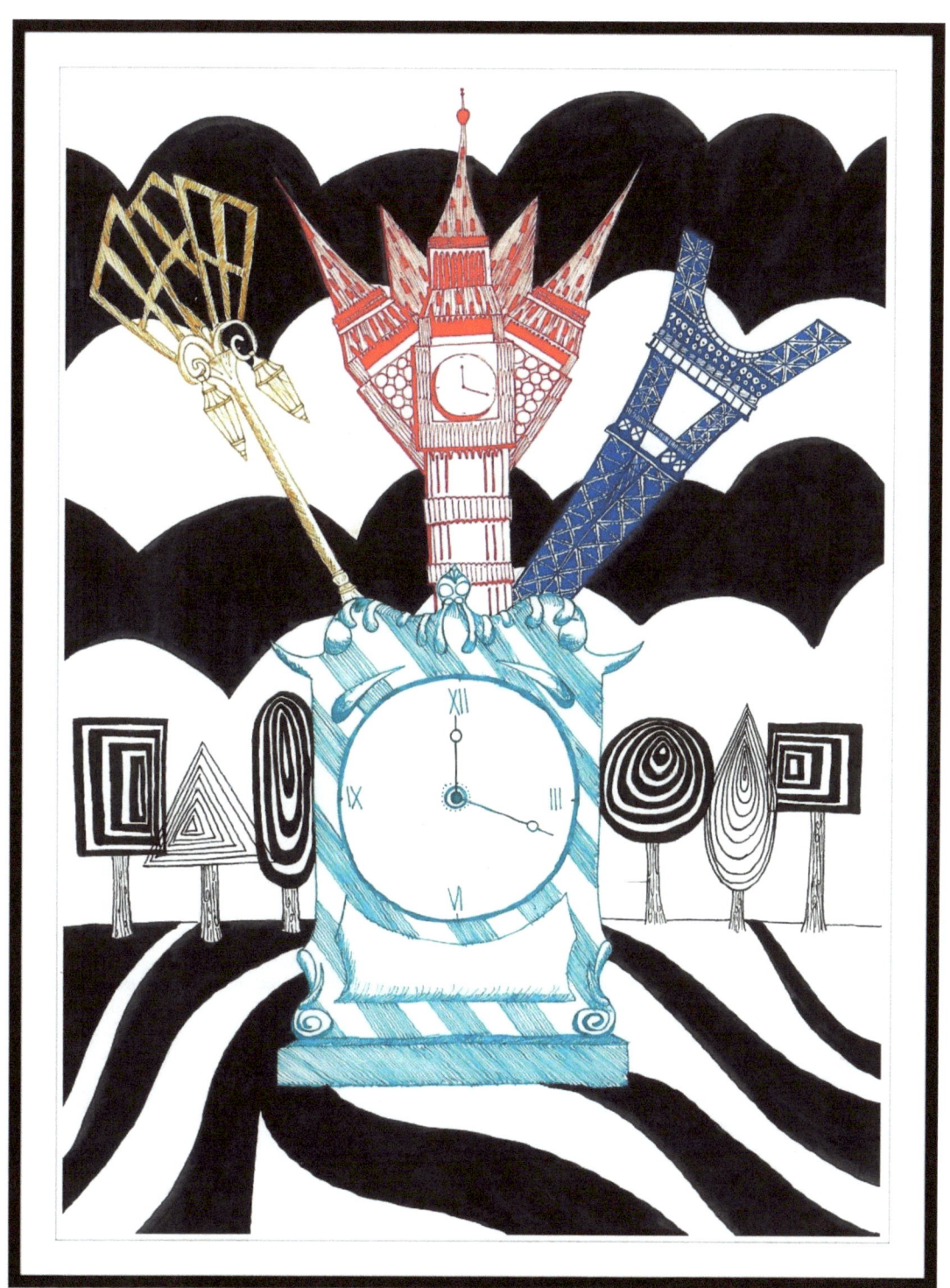

TIMELESS

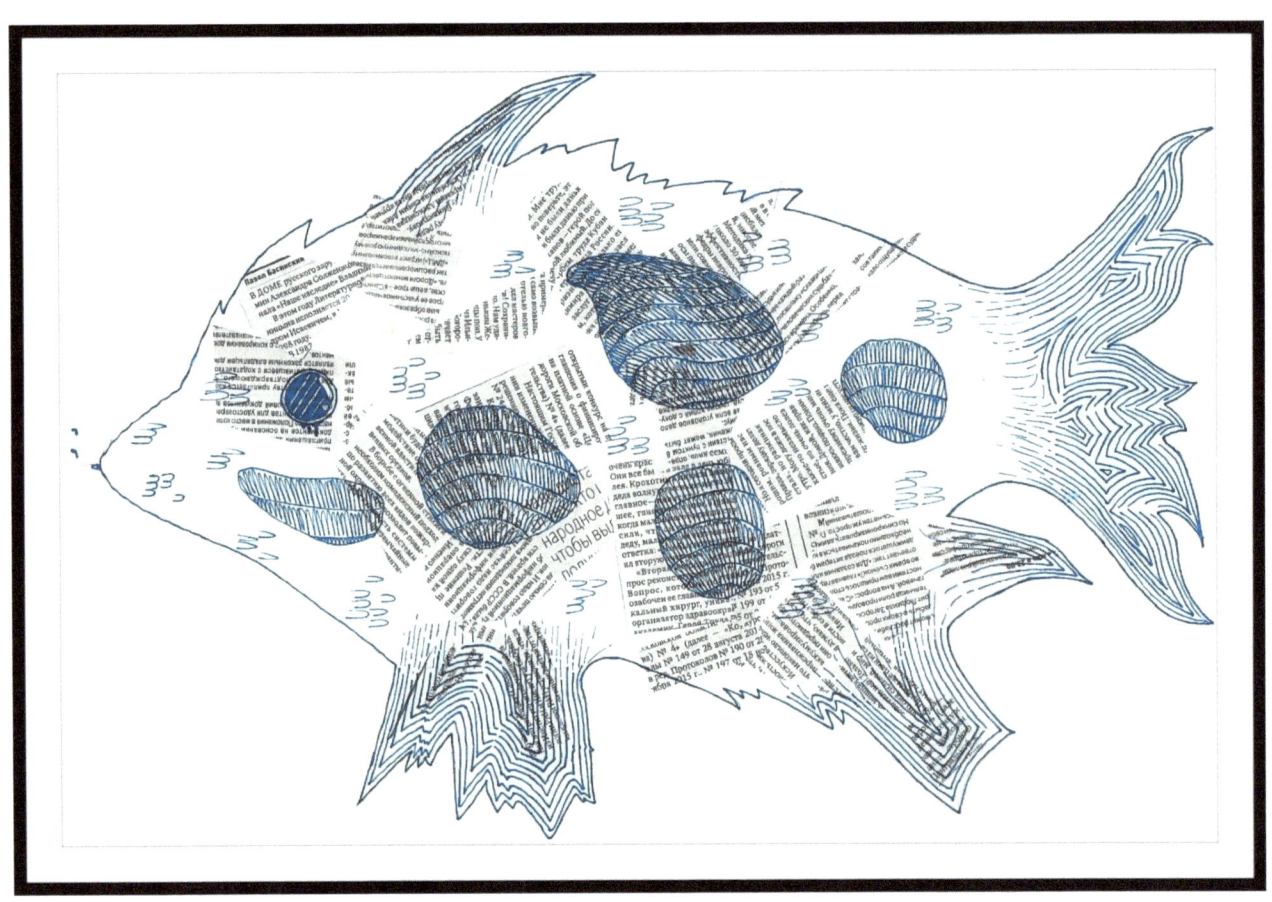

TIFFANY

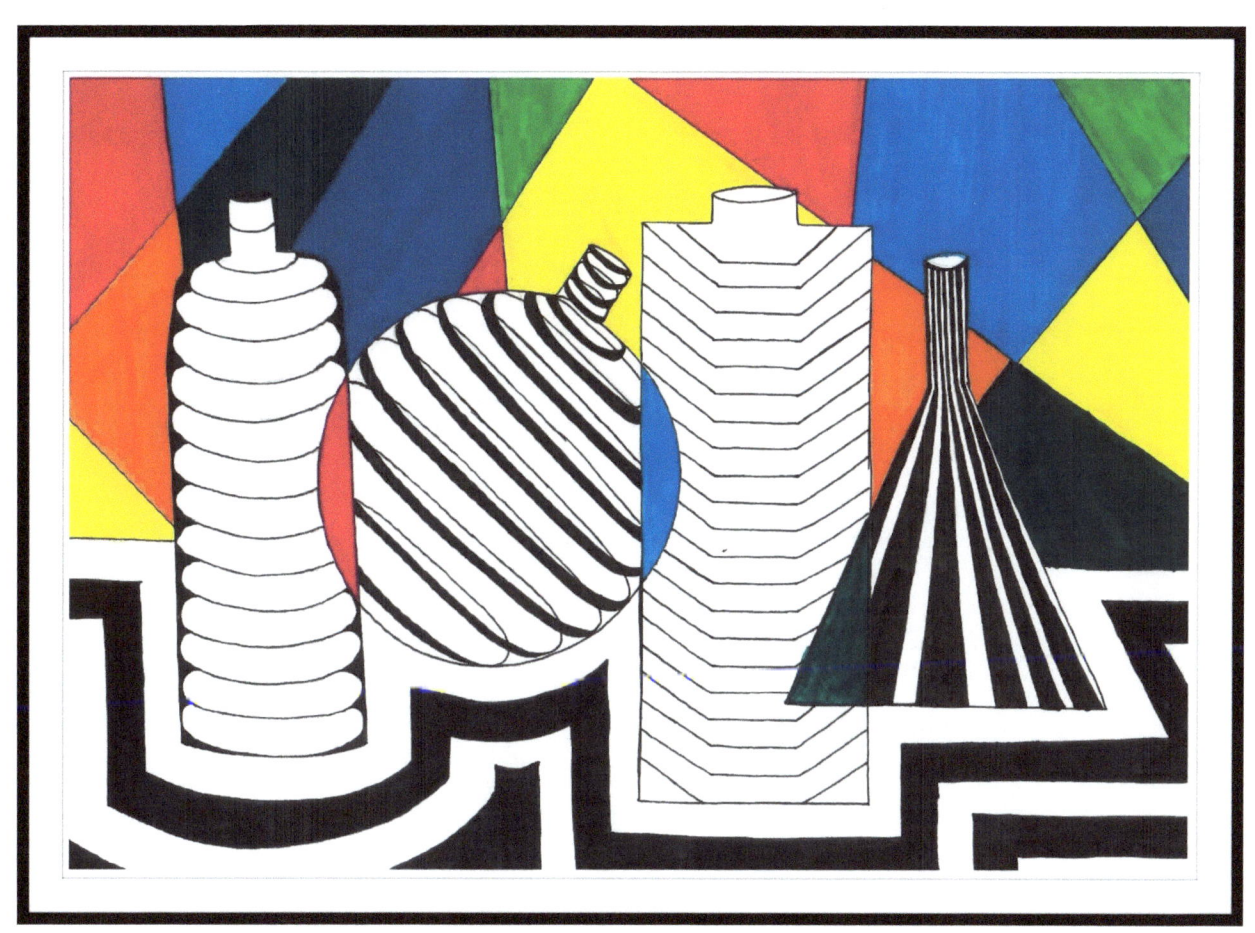

On Somebody's Shelf

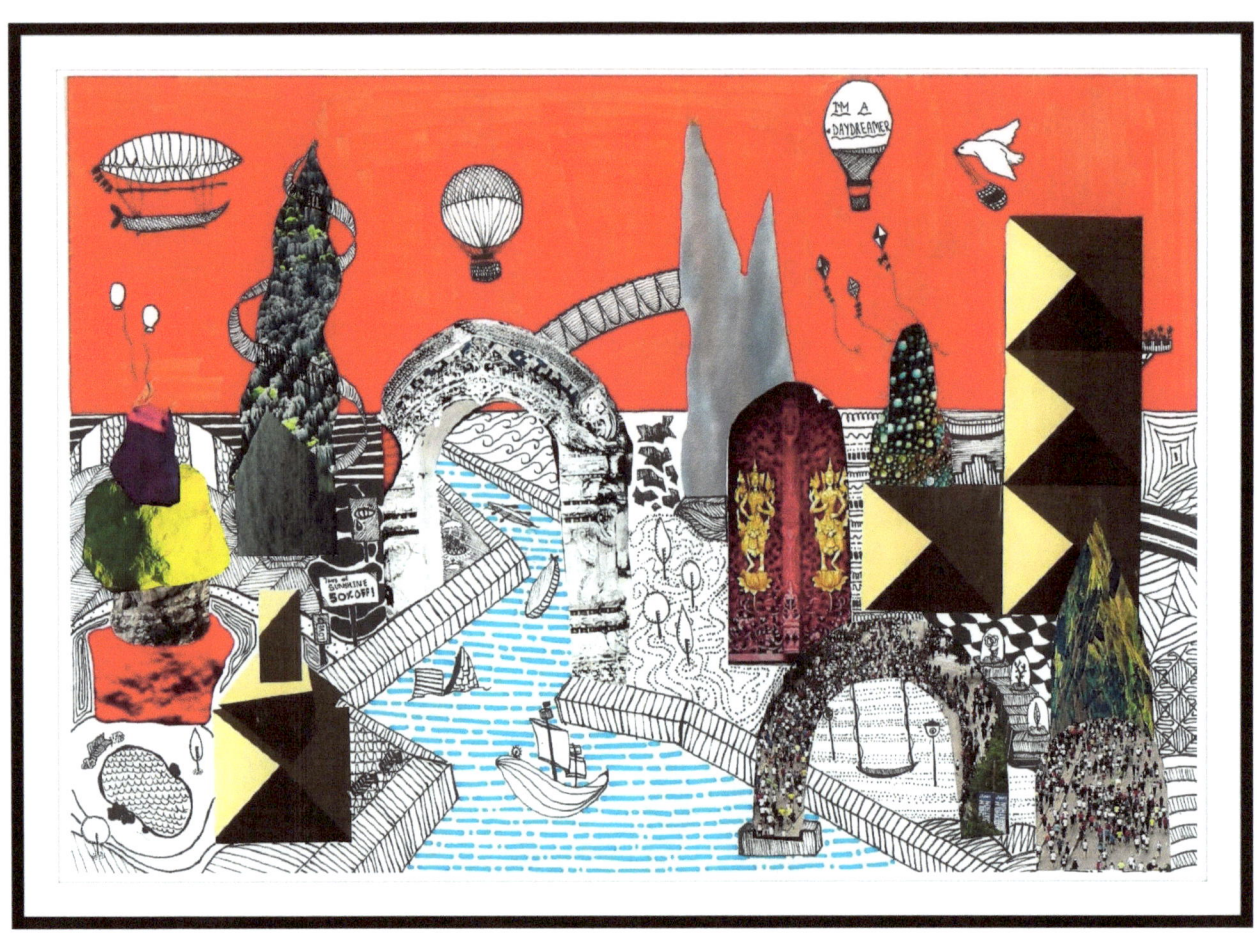

Where We Don't Exist

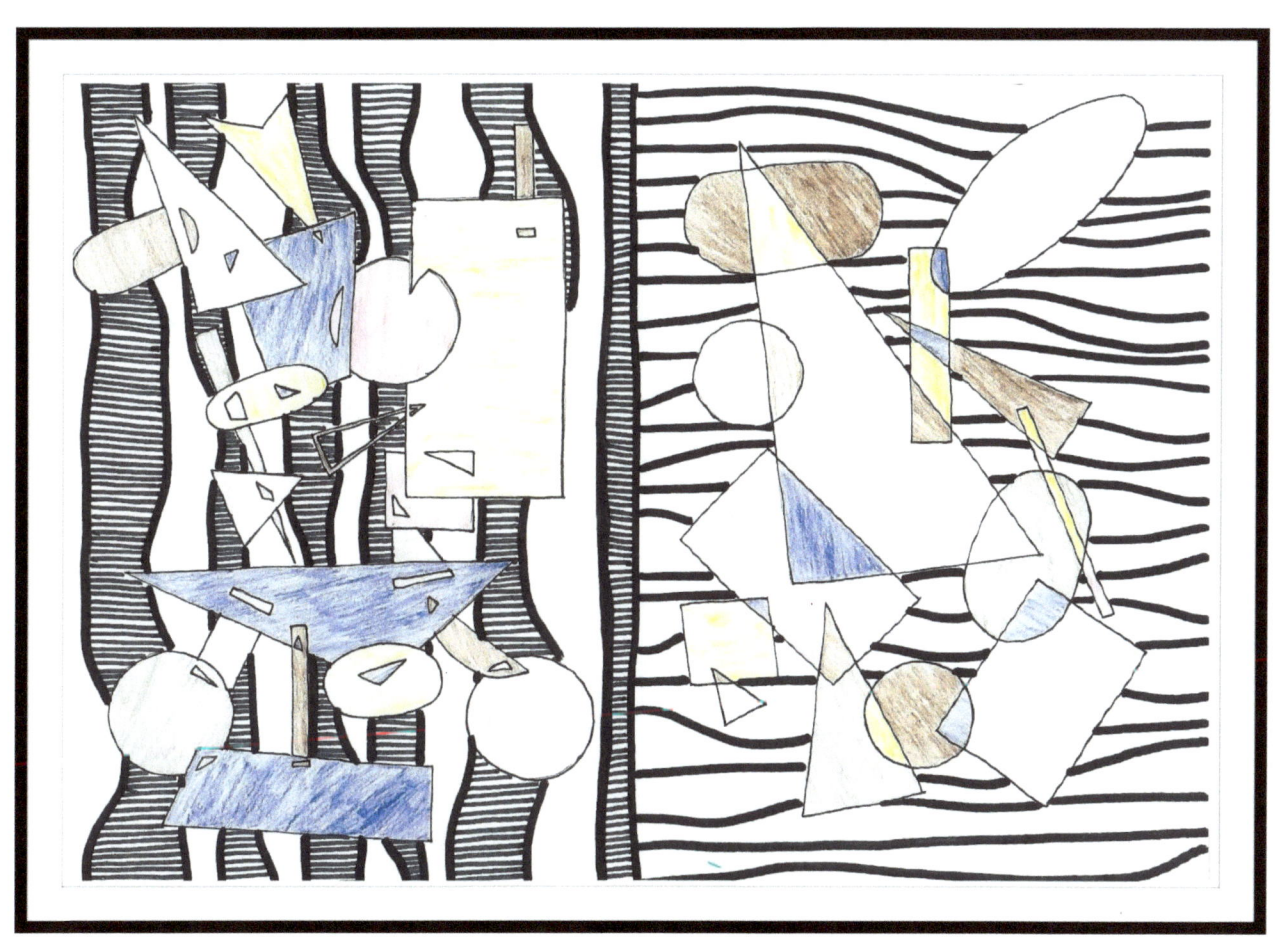

TUESDAY

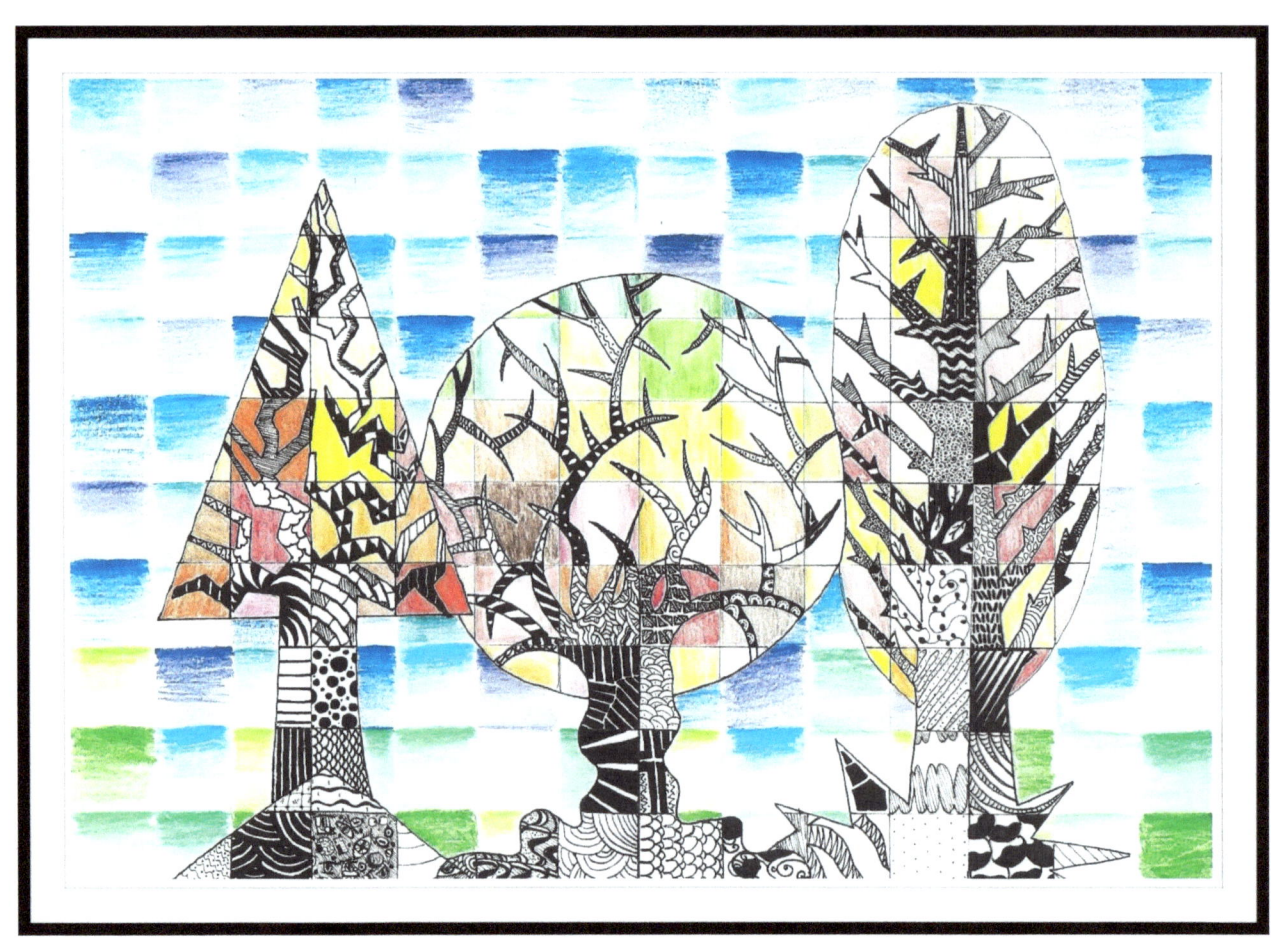

CURIOUSER AND
CURIOUSER

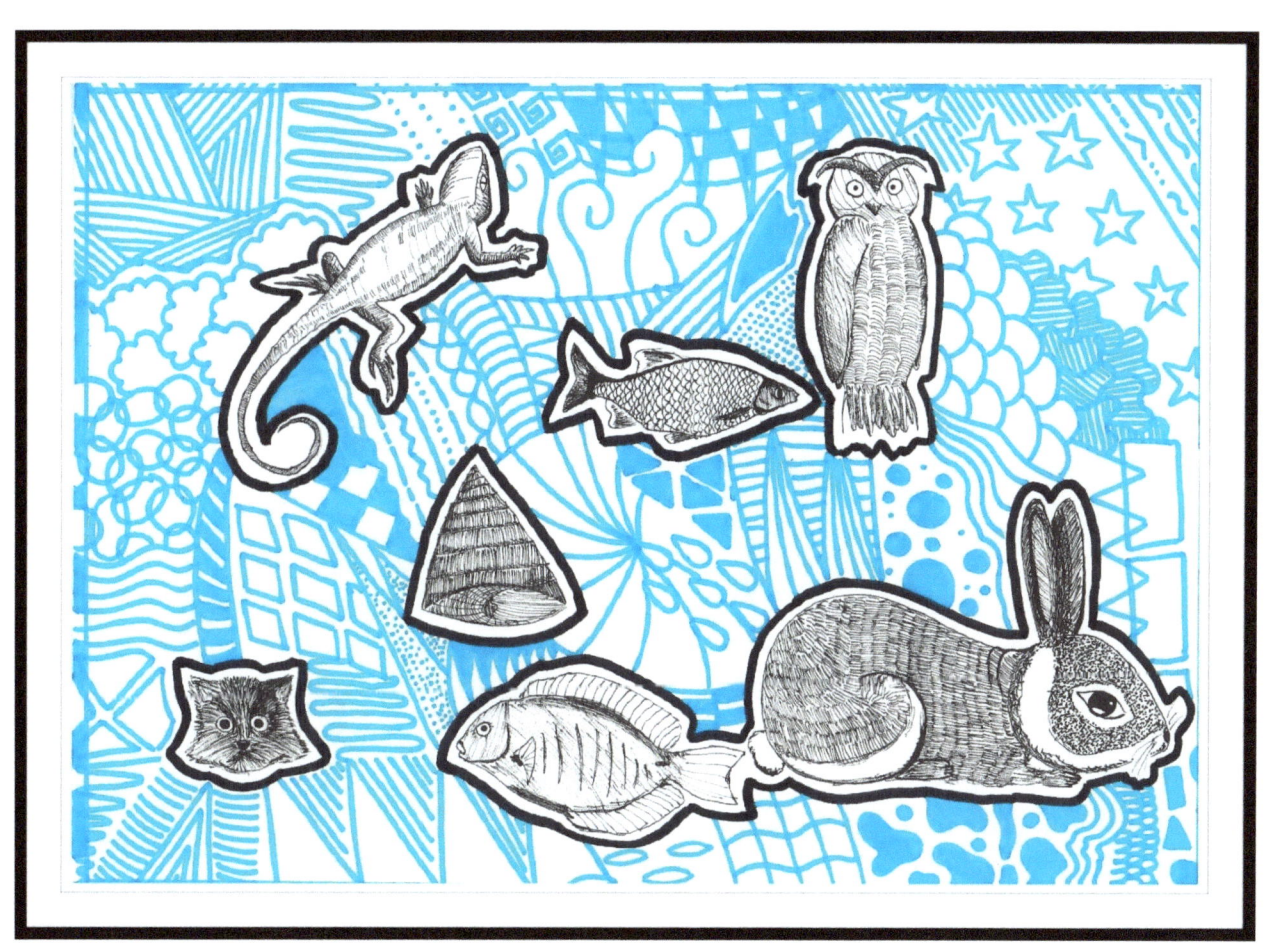

A World of Wonder

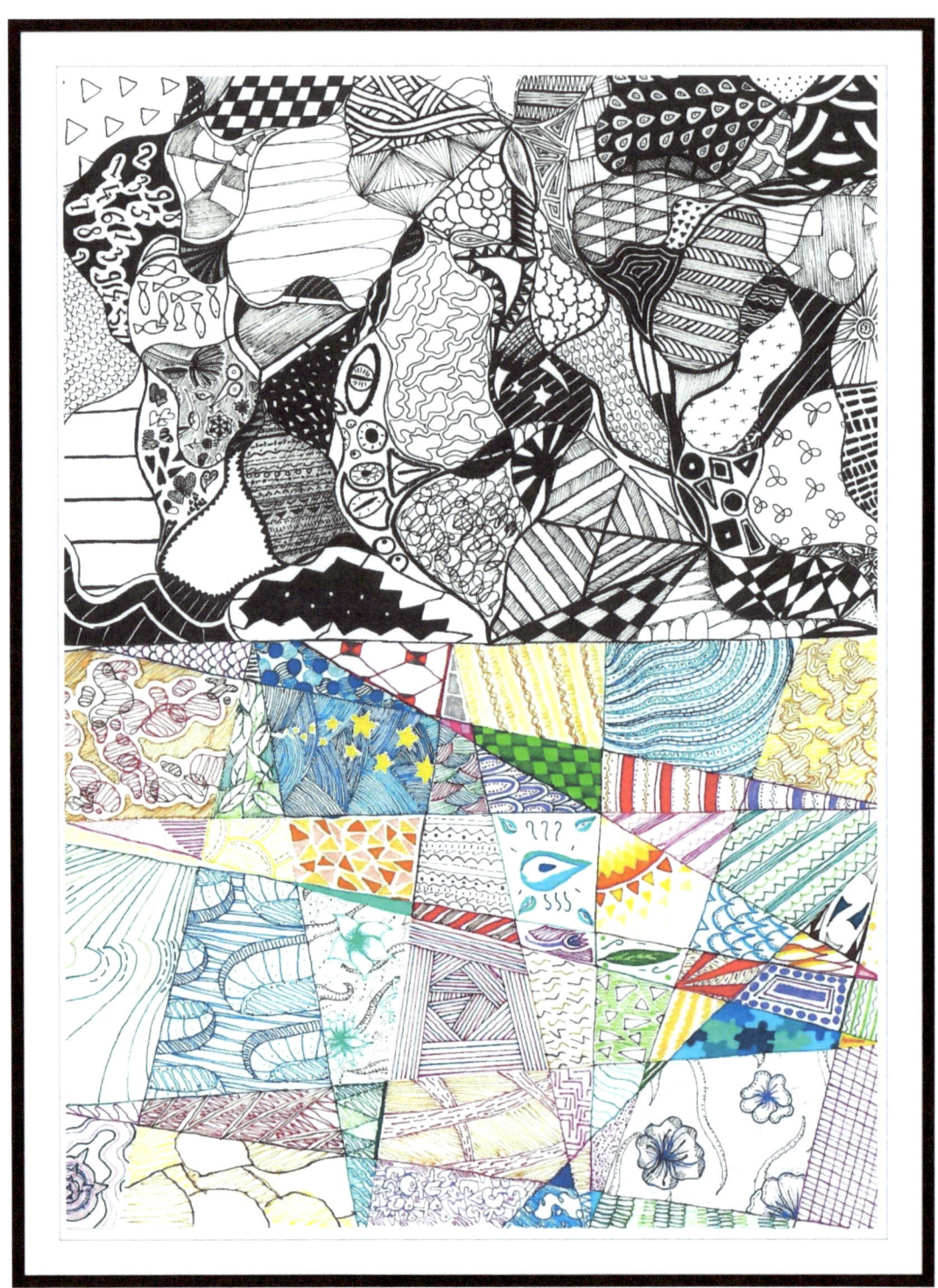

A Blur

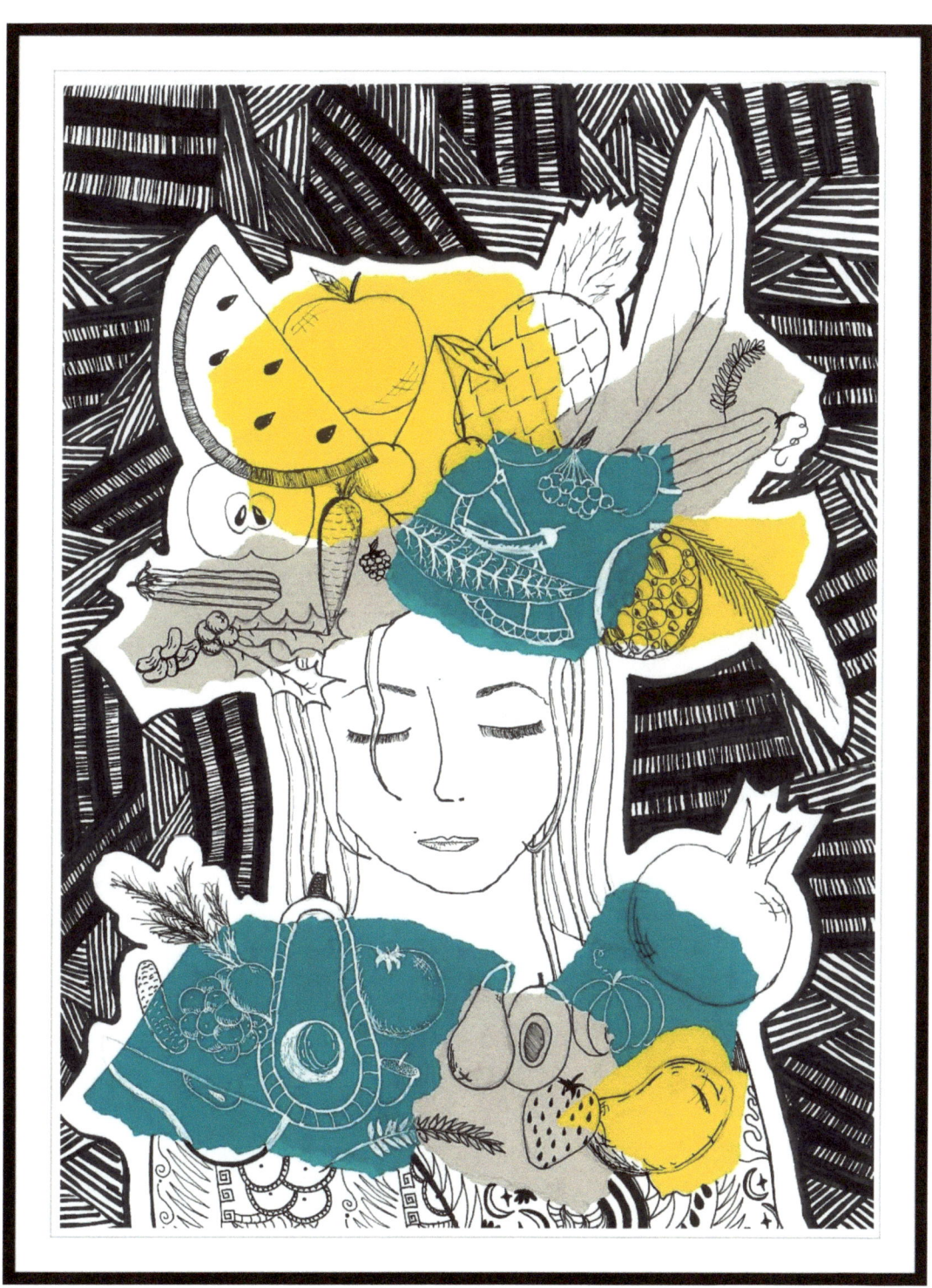

EXTREME VEGANISM

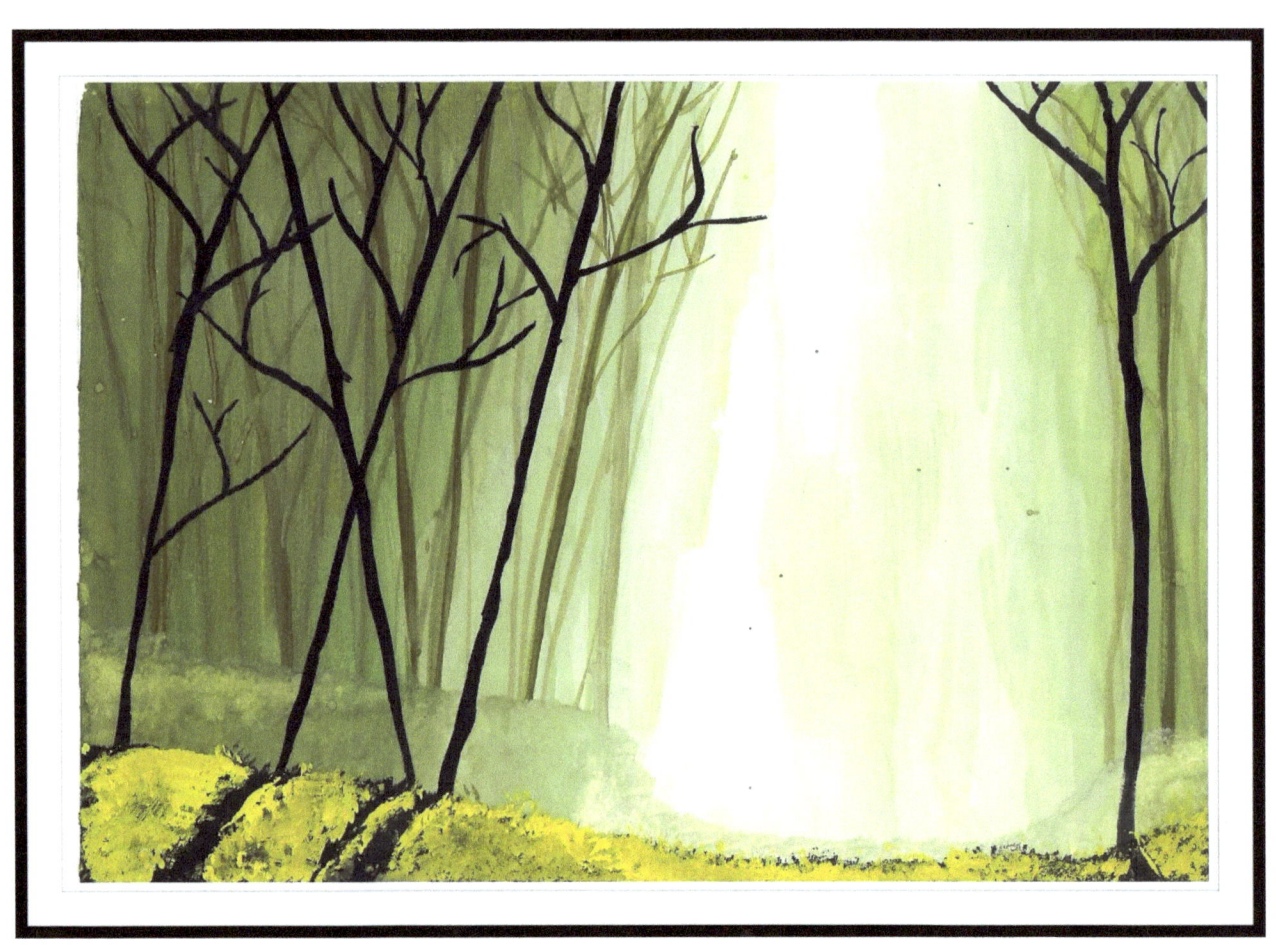

The Road Not Taken

Please contact Lika Gorsky
with all your questions and comments
@
gala72@bk.ru

www.ingramcontent.com/pod-product-compliance
Lightning Source LLC
Chambersburg PA
CBHW051832210526
45473CB00005B/1848